LESSONS FROM A BiRDBRAiN

SUMMER, OHiO

LESSONS FROM
A BiRDBRAiN
SUMMER, OHiO

Laura McDermott

TABLE OF CONTENTS

PREFACE

Why Did I Write This?

I have recently started birdwatching and bird photography as a hobby and find it enjoyable and rewarding. And yet at first, I found it overwhelming. I knew so little about birds beyond the sparrows and cardinals that eat at my feeder. The material I found online and the birders I met were knowledgeable, but I wanted more information about the species that I could find in this region. So, I started out writing this book as a beginner's guide to some of the birds you would commonly see in Ohio.

I have also been studying mindfulness and the pursuit of serenity. For me, there are direct connections between birdwatching and mindfulness. When I am outdoors with my binoculars and my camera, I have quiet time to slow down and be present to enjoy the amazing natural world. Plus, those activities give me the opportunity in the background to work through a challenge or troublesome situation while I take a break from my normal breakneck pace.

This book was born with the idea to combine these ideas of birdwatching and mindfulness lessons. My hope is that readers will encounter a concept they may have heard before but it will resonate differently. The saying "when the student is ready, the teacher appears" is powerful, and I hope that outcome will be encouraged by this book.

Who Is My Target Audience?

Ohio residents, beginning birders, young people, old people, and anyone who is open to personal growth will benefit from hearing these simple life lessons in a new way.

How to Use This Book

I would suggest reading a chapter per day for 21 days and reflecting on the "birdbrain lessons" throughout that time. Ideally, I'd suggest trying out birding during the same time. That can be simply a walk in your neighborhood, in a metro park or a trip to a wildlife area. I hope readers will achieve new insights along the way from the focus, fresh air and gentle exercise birding offers. For me, birding is like a 'walking meditation' that offers improved health, physical and mental and a sense of gratitude for the present and the natural world. I wrote 21 chapters to correlate with the number of days it takes to establish a new habit and hopefully, dear reader, you will get 'hooked' on birding as a path to mindfulness.

Will There Be More?

I have learned a great deal more about the birds I thought I already knew, so the answer to that question is "probably." I have enjoyed writing this and I may do other versions with perspectives from different seasons or different locations. I still have a day job but someday I hope to turn my birding hobby into a retirement gig leading birding tours or writing more books that will allow me to travel and enjoy more avian adventures.

So, if you enjoy this book, tell your friends, buy more books, and for heaven's sake, enjoy this very moment. The present is the gift we have today.

1

PiLEATED WOODPECKER

The Pileated Woodpecker is the largest woodpecker in North America at 16 to 18 inches, about the size of a crow. The woodpecker's tongue is twice the length of its bill and sticky to help catch insects in the holes the bird makes in trees.

You can typically find Pileated Woodpeckers in forests with large, mature trees and you will likely hear the birds before you see them. They make drumming noises to communicate infor-

mation about territory, mates, and food, and do not vocalize. You may think woodpeckers would get headaches from all of the banging, but they do not. Their brains are cushioned and their skulls are specially structured to spread the impact.

We human beings, however, do not have special cushions around our brains. We often "bang our heads against a wall" when we try to accomplish some task or goal that we have previously failed to achieve. For example, I get in that situation when I am trying to do something I've tried before that did not work, or asking someone else to do something that I cannot do.

To get unstuck, I find the best thing is to temporarily step away from the task at hand and come back another time with a different approach. And if my frustration is about changing another person's behavior, I have to realize the only person I can change is me. For example, let us say I have a friend who is always 15 minutes late for an activity. Rather than let that behavior annoy me every time I get together with him or her, I can show up at the time I know they will appear, or plan to do something fun in the 15 extra minutes until my friend arrives.

Who knows, maybe I can find a Pileated Woodpecker while I wait?

"JUST TRY NEW THINGS. DON'T BE AFRAID. STEP OUT OF YOUR COMFORT ZONES AND SOAR, ALL RIGHT?"
– MICHELLE OBAMA

Hoover Reservoir, Marsh Boardwalk Parking Lot, June 2020

2

RUBY-THROATED HUMMiNGBiRD

Ruby-throated hummingbirds are one of my two absolute favorite birds. They are one of the first species I studied when I became interested in birding, and the story of their annual migration is amazing. They come to the United States and Canada each spring to breed all the way from Central America, the Caribbean, and Mexico. Males head back south in July and females in September. Their trip across the Gulf of Mexico takes 18 to 20 hours, and there was once a myth that hummingbirds "hitched a ride" on other birds to accomplish the crossing. No, they are just that tough.

Ruby-throats are the only type of hummingbird you will see regularly in Ohio and throughout the eastern half of the United States. We occasionally also see the Rufous Hummingbird but if you notice a beautiful flash of green, it is most likely a ruby-throat. The birds are only seen in flight because their little feet are not very good for walking. Ruby-throats weigh about the same as a dime when they arrive in the spring, and once they have bulked up for the trip back south, they weigh about the same as a nickel.

Hummingbirds are fairly easy to attract to feeders. You can buy small hummingbird feeders online or in stores and put them up around Tax Day, April 15. The formula for "nectar" is one part sugar to four parts water. So, for example, I use one cup of water with one quarter cup of sugar. No red dye is needed for the mixture as long as your feeder has some red color to it. The birds can see red well and find feeders and flowers that way.

Around the time I started my hummingbird obsession, I also began training for half marathons. I was in my 40s and had no idea if I could run that far when I decided to try. But like everyone else, I followed a training plan, started with a doable goal, and built up distance over time. (I do not think hummingbirds have the luxury of following a training plan, but who knows?) And like a hummingbird who crosses the Gulf in an 18-hour stint, I was exhausted at the end of the race, and at the same time so happy to have reached my goal. After a few years, I started placing in races for my age group.

I respect hummingbirds for their speed and endurance and learned late in life that I share those qualities—at least a little— with the birds. But I did not make that connection until I was older. Each of us has wonderful qualities and strengths, some we know about early and some we find out later. Don't be afraid to ask your family and friends what qualities they see in you—sometimes we are just so used to our own talents, we don't fully appreciate them!

"MAKE THE MOST OF YOURSELF BY FANNING THE TINY, INNER SPARKS OF POSSIBILITY INTO FLAMES OF ACHIEVEMENT"– — GOLDA MEIR

3
GREATER YELLOWLEGS

Greater Yellowlegs are large shorebirds around 14 inches tall. They are summer visitors to Ohio and are named "yellowlegs" because, well, they have yellow legs. One thing I have noticed about how birds are named is the process is not always fancy, and in this case the experts went with a more obvious approach. As you might expect, "greaters" are typically larger than their cousins, the Lesser Yellowlegs.

I used my tripod to take these pictures and got some amazingly clear images. I was even able to take the picture from my phone, and I did not jiggle the camera by pressing the button. The Greater Yellowlegs is a good species to practice tripod photography on because the birds remain fairly still and do not seem to mind paparazzi like me.

Greater Yellowlegs have impressive migration patterns. They travel into Canada and Alaska to breed, come into the United States for summer, and then head down to Mexico and South America in fall and winter. So, think about that a minute—a bird that is up to your knee, if that, flies nearly 7000 miles during the course of a year! I'm not talking about using a plane and the birds take neither luggage nor cell phone. While you and I watch Netflix and wash our cars, these guys are doing some amazing travel.

The key for the greater yellowlegs, and for me, is to take things one day at a time. I find I can get completely overwhelmed if I look at a task that is huge like flying across a couple of continents.

But once I start to break the task down and check parts off my list, it becomes very doable. So, the next time you feel burdened by a major undertaking, think of our friends the yellowlegs and break down your task to just what you need to accomplish today, this hour, or this minute. You will arrive eventually.

"NOTHING IS PARTICULARLY HARD IF YOU DIVIDE IT INTO SMALL JOBS" – — Henry Ford

(previous) Ruby-throated Hummingbird (Lake Hope Nature Center, June 2020)
Greater Yellowlegs (Plains Wildlife Area, August 2020)

4

BLACK-CROWNED NiGHT HERON

This handsome bird can be found near bodies of water in Ohio and all over the world. This picture was taken on the Scioto River, close to downtown Columbus and I have seen Black-crowned night herons fairly regularly by Lake Erie. Their numbers in Ohio have been on the rise, probably due to conservation efforts. The Olentangy River has recently been allowed to return to a more natural state, resulting in more wetland areas that are favorable nesting sites for birds like the Black-crowned Night Heron.

Of all the birds I have studied, this one sports a wide and fascinating set of distinctive traits. According to the Animalia website, "A Black-crowned Night Heron will defend its feeding and nesting territories. The young may be aggressive, defecating or regurgitating on human intruders.... These birds have digestive acids that are so strong that bones dissolve in their stomachs." They are also the only birds that use 'tools' for fishing. They drop things in the water or stir it with their bills to lure fish.

I have started watching for birds and counting them while I walk or run. That helps me stay present in the moment and observant because my goal is to not miss what is going on around me. The first time I saw a Black-crowned Night Heron, I was surprised since I understood from one of my bird books that the heron was rare in that location. A few years ago, I would have missed the bird completely because my mind would have been going a million miles a minute. I was previously just getting the exercise done to check it off my to-do list and not being as mindful of my surroundings.

I highly recommend trying this tactic to help focus on the here and now, to increase the chances of seeing more birds, and keep yourself out of trouble. After all, if you inadvertently run into a juvenile Black-crowned Night Heron defending its territory, you might be in for an unpleasant (poopy) surprise!

> "DO NOT DWELL IN THE PAST, DO NOT DREAM OF THE FUTURE, CONCENTRATE THE MIND ON THE PRESENT MOMENT"
> – BUDDHA

Black-crowned Night Heron (Scioto Trail, June 2021)
(next) Mute and Trumpeter Swans (Arbors of Watermark, Columbus and Killdeer Plains Wildlife Area, July/August 2020)

5

MUTE AND TRUMPETER SWANS

First of all, I had no idea swans came to Ohio on a fairly regular basis until recently. Where did I think they lived? I had never thought much about it but certainly not here. Maybe I thought they only lived in fairy tales. Hmmm.

So in my defense of not knowing, the Mute Swan in the left picture is native to Europe and the far north of Africa. And it is actually considered an invasive species. That sounds pretty harsh for such a pretty bird but apparently they can take over and chase other birds out based on their size and levels of aggression. They can grow to five feet long with a wingspan of seven to eight feet and weigh up to 25 pounds. (As compared to a hummingbird at top weight of 'a nickel' it would take 4,536 hummingbirds to make the weight of one Mute Swan). Mute Swans were imported from Europe in the mid 1800s to beautify parks and zoos and some escaped and established breeding populations.

The Trumpeter Swan in the picture on the right is native to North America. Many states and organizations have sought to protect them after they were nearly hunted to extinction in the early 1900s. In 1932, fewer than 70 trumpeters were known to exist worldwide. In 1950, a new population of trumpeters was discovered in Alaska and they are now up to around 16,000 birds in North America of which, 500 live in the midwest. So seeing these birds thriving here in Ohio was a precious discovery. (fws.gov)

Now let's talk about their names, mute and trumpeter. As is

often the case, the people in the bird naming department gave us some good clues to tell the two apart if we are not familiar with the distinctions in appearance. Mute Swan calls are more hoarse and muffled than other swans. And they make whistling, snorting and hissing sounds in their communication with their young. The Trumpeter Swan calls are louder and sounds like (can you guess yet)?...a trumpet.

In the case of swans in North America, it seems ironic that the louder Trumpeter Swans have had a tougher road than the quieter Mute Swans.

These two species of swans remind me that there are times I should trumpet and times I should remain mute. I have tended to be on the quieter side for much of my life and am now learning to speak up for my own happiness and serenity. I'm reminded of a couple of my favorite quotes:

> "YOU GET IN LIFE WHAT YOU HAVE THE COURAGE TO ASK FOR"
> – NANCY SOLOMAN

> "THE MOST COURAGEOUS ACT IS STILL TO THINK FOR YOURSELF. ALOUD."
> – COCO CHANEL

6

BROWN BOOBY

I debated about including this picture and photo because in my lifetime I doubt I will see another Brown Booby in Ohio. So be warned—I cannot offer suggestions about where to go in the Buckeye State to see one of these precious birds. The Brown Booby is typically found in the Caribbean—and is common there like crows or vultures are here—but the bird is rarely seen here beyond the Atlantic and Pacific Ocean coastlines. This was the first recorded sighting in Ohio.

Bird nuts like me came in from all over the United States to get a chance to see this bird. When I arrived in the parking lot, there were probably 25 other people there with telescopes, binoculars, and high-powered cameras. I took a trail down to the water where the bird had been sighted and had to wait my turn in a small line of people to get close enough to take pictures. People with cameras and tripods were in the water to get the perfect shot.

This is a juvenile bird based on the overall dull brown feathers. A mature adult will have a distinct white chest and belly and darker brown contrasting upper feathers. Boobies are powerful and agile in flight but challenged by takeoffs and landings. They use perches like this dead tree and high winds to assist in their takeoffs. When they dive for fish, the birds plunge nearly straight down from a height of 30 to 50 feet.

Perhaps the most fun part of this bird sighting, besides its rarity, are the jokes that can be made about its name. One of my friends suggested this might be a male who came to Ohio after a female. I responded, "He's come a long way for a nice booby!" Another birding friend and I discussed putting "Booby or Bust" on the windows of their vehicle when making the trip up to see the wayward bird. The name actually comes from the Spanish word "bobo" meaning stupid or daft. Early explorers thought the birds' clumsiness on takeoff and their lack of fear of humans indicated small bird brains.

I, along with the hundreds of other birders who shared in the excitement and joy, feel extremely lucky to have had the opportunity to see this bird in Ohio. Birding is a simple hobby that offers great happiness that can be easily shared.

> "THOUSANDS OF CANDLES CAN BE LIGHTED FROM A SINGLE CANDLE AND THE LIFE OF THE CANDLE WILL NOT BE SHORTENED. HAPPINESS NEVER DECREASES BY BEING SHARED."
> – BUDDHA

Brown Booby (Nimisila Reservoir, Akron, August 2020)

7

PURPLE MARTiN

Purple Martins are the largest swallow in the United States with a wingspan of up to 15 inches. (That is nearly the width of both my hands and definitely bigger than I realized!). They spend most of their lives in the air, eating and drinking while in flight. Purple Martins are called "aerial insectivores," meaning they catch and eat insects 160 to 500 feet above the ground. I have also seen them at dusk drinking from the surface of a lake. Unfortunately, they are one of the groups of birds on the decline in our state and country due to the use of pesticides employed to kill the bugs the Purple Martins eat.

On the bright side, many humans are trying to help and there are entire charitable organizations set up to protect the Purple Martin population. People also help by building nesting houses like the one in this picture. Purple Martins thrive in this communal setting with hundreds of birds living in this lovely apartment complex on a body of water, Delaware Lake, which offers an abundant food source. A set up such as that is called a "roosting colony," and the largest was estimated to house 700,000 birds according to thespruce.com. In contrast to these high-rise buildings, Native Americans have long encouraged Purple Martins to build near their settlements by offering the birds hollow gourds as single-family housing units.

Despite the name, Purple Martin feathers are actually bluish black and look purple, black, blue, or even green depending on the lighting. You can tell by the birds' notched tails that they are swallows as compared to other birds like the chimney swift. Females are grayer and have some patterning on their chests and bellies.

Purple Martins are beautiful birds especially when you glimpse them up close and get to see their stunning plumage. Until you stop and look, you may have discounted them as just another dark bird. I have been reading about how engrained it is in our culture to equate a dark appearance with evil intentions. Think of terms like "blackmail" and "blacklisted." I am trying to raise my awareness and challenge my thinking when it comes to darkness and light in all living creatures. The Purple Martin helps me appreciate how humans can help in our fight against racism as well as increase the populations of these delightful dark birds.

"THE DARKNESS AROUND US MIGHT SOMEWHAT LIGHT UP IF WE WOULD FIRST PRACTICE USING THE LIGHT WE HAVE IN THE PLACE WE ARE." – HENRY S. HASKINS

8
AMERiCAN HERRiNG GULL

Herring Gulls are the larger of the two seagulls we frequently see in Ohio. They are often mixed in with flocks of the more common ring-billed gull. You can occasionally see a Herring Gull inland on smaller lakes and rivers but the largest number of these birds is found on Lake Erie. They frequent garbage dumps as scavengers.

The American Herring Gull is also called the Smithsonian Gull. The European Herring gull also occasionally shows up on our country's Atlantic coast, but that species is not thought to be closely related to the American type. Wikipedia mentions that "the taxonomy of the herring gull group is very complicated, controversial and uncertain." I will let ornithologists—the bird biologists—work that out.

Juvenile Herring Gulls look nothing like the adults. They are much browner and take four years to mature into an adult gull's pure white feathers. Experienced birders can look at a brown herring gull and tell if it is a first or second year juvenile by the slight color variation in its feathers, but I'm not yet that astute to make that distinction. Herring Gulls have been known to live as long as 34 years. In the bird world, that is pretty old.

I did not realize this was a Herring Gull picture until I looked more closely and saw red on its bill. A black marking would have instead indicated it was a Ring-billed. I can also tell a Herring Gull apart by size when they are with Ring-bills that are much smaller and lighter. I have found that location is everything—that is a major clue when trying to figure out what bird I am seeing.

The weekend I took this picture I was out hoping to see warblers with some friends. I had seen a ton of warblers the prior weekend in that location. But the warblers, alas, had moved on into Canada. I set out with an expectation of seeing warblers and did not. Instead, I got this great picture of a herring gull and the weather was lovely. I recall the weekend with my friends fondly and did not let the lack of warblers erode my enjoyment of the experience. I kept the proper perspective.

"IF YOU CHANGE THE WAY YOU LOOK AT THINGS, THE THINGS YOU LOOK AT CHANGE." - Wayne Dyer

(previous) Purple Martin (Delaware State Park, July 2020)
(below) American Herring Gull (East Harbor State Park, May 2020)

9
BALTIMORE ORIOLE

In the first few days of May, we saw the first Baltimore Oriole of the year at a local metro park in Columbus, and by the end of May, they were everywhere. The bird's bright orange flash is an exciting welcome to spring each year.

Baltimore Orioles are members of the blackbird family and were named after Lord Baltimore, apparently a dude who liked his orange threads. They are one of two types we can see here in Ohio, the other being Orchard Orioles. Baltimores are fairly common, whereas orchards are less widespread. I have seen only one this year, but I do not spend a lot of time in orchards, so that might be a factor.

You can attract Baltimores to backyard feeders using a variety of sweet treats. They like oranges cut in half and some people use grape jelly to attract these birds. Orioles also enjoy hummingbird feeders. I have seen Baltimore orioles on hummingbird feeders on at least three occasions this year. The birds are more likely to stay and set up a nesting site if you get your feeders out early. Baltimores like water and the color orange, so putting an orange feeder by a birdbath may increase your chances of attracting orioles.

The last two weeks of May are warbler season in Ohio and I was intent on finding as many of them as I could. I saw so many Baltimore Orioles that I started thinking, "Oh, it is just another oriole," when a flash of orange attracted my eye. But now, as I write this in early September, the orioles have left for their southern winter residences. Some winter in Florida, but most travel to Mexico and South America. The orioles are here one day and gone the next.

I sometimes take for granted that which is plentiful in my life. This can happen with anything—people and relationships, travel, even our abundant electricity and water in the United States. The pandemic of 2020 has temporarily halted many things I took for granted. What has happened in the world in recent months reminds me to avoid taking for granted everything around me and pause to appreciate the preciousness of it all.

> "APPRECIATE WHAT YOU HAVE BEFORE IT TURNS INTO WHAT YOU HAD." – ZIAD ABDELNOUR

Baltimore Oriole (East Harbor State Park, August 2021)

TURKEY VULTURES

I took these pictures on one of those super-hot Ohio July days. I did not go out birding expecting to find anything in particular, and I saw the usual suspects around Delaware Lake. Nevertheless, here was an unexpected sight! I had not previously seen Turkey Vultures hanging out quite like this.

You may think Turkey Vultures are not the most gorgeous birds in the state and most of your neighbors would agree. The birds have bald heads and close up look like a turkey, hence the

name. A vulture's lack of feathers on its head helps prevent food from sticking to it. This is a particularly smart feature for hungry scavengers that stick their heads in carcasses.

Turkey Vultures have a powerful sense of smell to find their food, which is an unusual trait in the bird world. Vultures are not capable of killing prey but instead can detect carrion—dead animal carcasses—up to a mile away. Turkey Vulture brains have the largest smell receptors of all birds, but they can only smell carcasses that are 12 to 24 hours old. Vultures help clean up the environment and prevent rot and disease. Go, vultures!

I have often seen Turkey Vultures and their less numerous relatives, the Black Vultures, in flight over fields. They soar in an easy way, probably searching for a snack. But the large group of them perched in trees was a new experience. The birds group together during migration in the spring and fall. According to the Chattahoochee Nature Center, in the picture above the vultures are "sunbathing" to increase their body temperature after a cool night.

We often gather with others very similar to us in appearance and thought. I bet these vultures think their buddies are quite gorgeous, no matter what we humans say. I feel the same way when I get together with my friends and family who love me no matter how I look that day. Sometimes we need that sense of belonging that comes from being with our "peeps," even if we have a little food on our faces.

> "FAMILY ISN'T ALWAYS BLOOD. IT'S THE PEOPLE IN YOUR LIFE WHO WANT YOU IN THEIRS, THE ONES WHO ACCEPT YOU FOR WHO YOU ARE, THE ONES WHO WOULD DO ANYTHING TO SEE YOU SMILE AND WHO LOVE YOU NO MATTER WHAT."
> – PAUL WALKER

Turkey Vultures (Delaware State Park, July 2020)
(next) Indigo Bunting (Kelleys Island State Park Boardwalk, July 2020)

11

INDiGO BUNTiNG

The Indigo Bunting's summer song is one that you have heard more times than you likely realize. The bird sings from the tops of trees to attract a mate and that call helps me spot the species when I am out birding. The Indigo Bunting is in the cardinal family and its single chirping calls sound similar to the sounds of the Northern Cardinal, our state bird. From afar, buntings can look black—and their feathers *are* actually black—but light diffusion results in a beautiful turquoise appearance when the feathers are touched by the rays of the sun.

Indigo Buntings can be found throughout Ohio and the eastern United States where the birds breed in summer. In winter, the buntings head back to the eastern coast of Mexico and Costa Rica. They—and many other birds—navigate using the stars! Who knew? Experiments have been done with buntings where they are placed in a planetarium where star patterns can be simulated and the birds are still able to orient themselves based on the patterns.

During summer, Indigo Buntings eat insects and spiders as well as weed seeds. They are considered beneficial to farmers for that reason. The bunting's diet also provides the protein needed for nesting and raising young. During migration and in the winter, they switch their diet to berries, buds, and seeds.

I sometimes spot Indigo Buntings during my early morning

walks and runs along the Scioto River. On a recent jaunt, I was conducting my normal bird count and thought I heard a cardinal chirping. For whatever reason, I decided to take a closer look with my binoculars and was treated to a bunting sighting in the early morning sun. It was truly breathtaking, and I appreciated that I did not miss that experience. Now when I hear that distinctive chirp, I am more careful to stop and look.

Our human brains have developed an amazing capacity to unconsciously catalog and categorize what is going on around us. With the amount of visual and audio stimuli going on at any one time, our brains have to be selective so we can focus and concentrate. But that sensible adaptation can cause us to miss out on many things if we don't tune in and are mindful so as not to miss the Indigo Buntings of the day. We often live our lives on autopilot. We wake up, go to work, make dinner, go to bed, sleep, rinse, and repeat. Birding allows me to shut off the autopilot and tune in the sounds, sights, and beauty of the world.

"WE ALL MAKE BASIC ASSUMPTIONS ABOUT THINGS IN LIFE, BUT SOMETIMES THOSE ASSUMPTIONS ARE WRONG. WE MUST NEVER TRUST IN WHAT WE ASSUME, ONLY IN WHAT WE KNOW."
— Darren Shan

12

GREAT BLUE HERON

This is Helen. She is a Great Blue Heron perched over the Big Darby River. I was standing on a bridge close to the middle of downtown Plain City and saw Helen waiting for her breakfast to come along. Or maybe she had already eaten—I could not really tell. You'll notice Helen appears to have only one leg.

Great Blue Herons like Helen are considered common and can be seen near open water all over Ohio and across North America. They are the largest of the continent's herons, and according to Wikipedia, "are only surpassed by the Goliath Heron" in size. They can have a wingspan of 66 to 79 inches, a height of 45 to 54 inches, and weigh only four to eight pounds.

These hardy birds feed in shallow waters and some remain here through our cold Ohio winters. They are able to stick around as long as we do not experience a particularly harsh winter that freezes over the shallow rivers and lakes where the herons feed. You may have seen herons on the hunt, walking slowly in the shallow water, and then suddenly jabbing their prey with their beaks. Small fish make up most of Helen's diet and she will also happily eat aquatic insects, frogs, rodents, and even other small birds!

As with many birds, I am alerted to a Great Blue Heron's presence by its call. The call of a heron is unique and memorable, and sounds like a hoarse, deep croak. I have heard these birds squawking at night and been startled by—and startled them—in the early morning. My first reaction to hearing the heron's call is to scan the open water, although I have sometimes found the birds perched high up in trees, like Helen is in this picture.

You may be wondering why I decided to give Helen a name. I spent a long time photographing that morning and got to know her pretty well by the time she flew away. I was also impressed by her resilience, missing a limb did not seem to hamper her. I am just learning to use my camera and I end up zooming in and out multiple times from multiple angles before I get the picture I want. Life is a bit like that, too. I find it helpful to sometimes "zoom out" to look at a situation, especially if it is troublesome or appears to be a handicap, to get a better view of the big picture. Any one moment or challenge in my life is bound to be fleeting. I am working to improve my ability to shift my perspective—to zoom in and out and look at things from different angles in order to continue to grow and maintain serenity.

> "TO KEEP OUR FACES TOWARD CHANGE AND BEHAVE LIKE FREE SPIRITS IN THE PRESENCE OF FATE IS STRENGTH UNDEFEATABLE."
> – HELLEN KELLER

RUDDY DUCK

When I originally wrote this chapter, I thought this was a female bufflehead. One of my early reviewers pointed out it is a Ruddy Duck, and although he was too kind to say, it is a male. This particular bird was a frequent visitor to the calm waters inside the fishing pier at Kelleys Island State Park. Along with being this guy's name, Ruddy Ducks also have a tavern and cabins named after them. It is not potentially as interesting as the Bufflehead name (because its head is large and looks like a buffalo?), but it is noteworthy all the same.

Many birding resources include information about breeding

and nesting behaviors, which typically do not help me identify species, so I don't pay a ton of attention to the mating details. The Ruddy Duck's courtship behavior, however, is fascinating. To attract a mate, a male will swim around the apple of his eye; slap his chest with his broad, flat bill; and then run on the water. The male scoots across the water and if the lovely lady accepts him, she stretches her neck, and opens her bill. That is considerably more work than taking someone out to dinner!

Ruddy Ducks are diving ducks, which made getting this picture somewhat challenging. Every time I would get my camera to focus, he would plunge back down into the water to forage for aquatic plants, insect larvae, and fish eggs. These ducks are native to North and South America and are common in the West. Ruddy Ducks have also migrated to Europe and are considered an invasive species there.

This Ruddy Duck hung out for several days and I got the chance to watch him feeding. At other times, he would remain still and was, apparently, resting or sleeping. He also spent time preening and fluffing his feathers. I found it fascinating to watch him cycle through his day and balance his time. Balance in activity is for me an essential element of my sense of serenity, and like many of us, one I often forget to manage. I can "over index" the feeding part (working for financial freedom and security) and neglect my need for rest and self-care. The moral of the Ruddy Duck's story is a reminder to treat myself to the rest and restoration I need to remain balanced.

"BALANCE IS THE KEY TO EVERYTHING. WHAT WE DO, THINK, SAY, EAT, FEEL, THEY ALL REQUIRE AWARENESS, AND THROUGH THIS AWARENESS WE CAN GROW."

– KOI FRESCO

(previous) Great Blue Heron (Plain City, August 2020)
(left) Ruddy Duck (Kelleys Island State Park Pier, July 2020)

14
TREE SWALLOW

Tree Swallows are early spring migratory arrivals, showing up as early as March. With the bad weather we had this year, however, they changed their travel plans and I saw this one in early May. Once they arrive, you will typically see lots of these birds gathering in flocks called a "stand" of swallows. They also leave relatively early in the year with most of them gone by August. Some Tree Swallows spend the winter as far north as the Carolinas and others go for a more tropical vibe, heading to the Gulf Coast, Cuba, or Guatemala. They switch their diet to berries over the winter which is one of the reasons they are able to stay farther north than other swallows.

Tree Swallows are enjoyable to watch in flight. They are agile, often making sharp turns, quick ascents, and steep descents to capture insects in flight. They occasionally go after feathers in the air which is thought to be a playful behavior. Their call is an enjoyable gurgling sound that I look forward to each spring.

I cannot tell by sight if this is a female or a male in the photo. Both sexes sport a lovely turquoise blue-green look with a white belly, although females have slightly more brown plumage and therefore appear less blue than males. To be safe, I named this one Chris. In reality, it does not matter. I was recently reading a passage encouraging each of us to embrace our feminine and masculine qualities because we all have both. I thought about that for a minute, first discounted the observation, but then realized it is very true. I have a competitive streak, especially when it comes to work and running, that would be considered more masculine. And I am cool with that. I am nurturing and supportive, too, which are considered more feminine traits. That is also cool. *In fact, what if I adopt a pen name of "Chris," too? Then, dear reader, you will not know if I am female or male!*

"LIKE A FRENCH POEM IS LIFE; BEING ONLY PERFECT IN STRUCTURE WHEN THE MASCULINE RHYMES MINGLED WITH THE FEMININE ARE." – HENRY WADSWORTH LONGFELLOW

Tree Swallow (Kelleys Island, May 2021)

PROTHONOTARY WARBLER

The Prothonotary Warbler is tied with the Ruby-throated Hummingbird as my favorite of all birds. Warblers were one of the first species I studied extensively when I started birding. I thought—and still think—it is the loveliest of the lovely.

In general, I enjoy the amazing story of migratory birds who summer in North America and winter in the Tropics. I also want to be a migratory bird spending Ohio's cold weather months in a warmer climate. I am working on that dream, but back to Prothonotary Warblers. They are primarily found in the eastern part

of the U.S. and winter in the West Indies, Central America, and South America.

Their primary habitat is wooded swampy areas and are the only warbler that nests in cavities. Their nests are sometimes taken over by Brown-headed Cowbirds and this has impacted the overall warbler population. Luckily, Prothonotary Warblers have a fan base of conservation-minded people who have built extra nesting boxes in favorable locations. As a result, the warbler population is considered stable and in some areas even thriving.

Hoover Reservoir, just south of Galena, is one site that has been so successful in its efforts to protect birds that people come from all over the world to study the reservoir's conservation program. Charlie Bombaci has led the effort for over 20 years to create a favorable breeding habitat for Prothonotary Warblers. He has put up over 250 nest boxes which has helped increase the number of local breeding warbler pairs by a factor of five since the early 2000s.

I stumbled upon the Hoover conservation area when I traveled there to meet a friend for a run and get a little birding in on the side. I was planning to go to a nearby boardwalk which was closed due to the COVID pandemic. I might never have known about this area if it were not for the unfortunate circumstance that derailed my original plans. Thankfully, I did not spend my morning seeing only a closed door.

"WHEN ONE DOOR CLOSES, ANOTHER DOOR OPENS, BUT WE SO OFTEN LOOK SO LONG AND SO REGRETFULLY UPON THE CLOSED DOOR THAT WE DO NOT SEE THE ONES WHiCH OPEN FOR US." – ALEXANDER GRAHAM BELL.

Prothonotary Warbler (Hoover Reservoir, May 2021)

16
DOUBLE-CRESTED CORMORANT

Cormorants are considered seabirds and the Double-crested ones we find in Ohio have a wide range in North America from Alaska to Florida and Mexico. They live along rivers and lakes, are here only in summer, and head to southern coastal areas each September, the lucky ducks. Wait—they are seabirds, not ducks!

You are probably wondering, "Hey, why are they called double-crested? I am not seeing it." During breeding season, these cormorants sport a small double-crest of black and white feathers. Next season, I will make a point of looking for and photographing said crest. I did look up a picture for reference and the crest looks quite attractive (!), like fluffy, white, really long eyebrows, or ear hair.

You will often only see the neck and head of a cormorant in the water as they swim low and spend a lot of time underwater, fishing. That made this picture all the more exciting to me to find them sunning themselves. Their feathers are not waterproof, and you will frequently see them spreading their wings to dry. Cormorants out of the water always remind me of the "crane pose" in *The Karate Kid*, if you have ever seen that 1984 movie. Up close, or with a camera or binoculars, you can see the skin on their cormorant necks and heads is yellowish orange.

I frequently see cormorants in trios and often think of Bob Marley's "Three Little Birds" song in my head. He sings, "Don't worry about a thing/'Cause every little thing gonna be all right."

That is wise counsel from Mr. Marley and these handsome sea-birds. Worry is not a worthwhile activity because it is just a projection of something that may or may not happen. So, if my mind starts to worry, I find my best approach is to get in touch with the feeling behind the problem and act, if and when it makes sense. Always try to heed the advice of these wise birds!

> "WHEN I LOOK BACK ON ALL THESE WORRIES, I REMEMBER THE STORY OF THE OLD MAN WHO SAID ON THIS DEATHBED THAT HE HAD A LOT OF TROUBLE IN HIS LIFE, MOST OF WHICH HAD NEVER HAPPENED."   – WINSTON CHURCHILL

Double-crested Cormorant (Scioto River Bike Trail, September 2020)

17
GREAT EGRET

I have taken many lovely photographs of Great Egrets in the last several months. These birds are, thankfully, plenty in number. Plus, they are easy to spot with their bright plumage along nearby rivers and lakes.

These stunning birds serve as the logo of the National Audubon Society and represent the power of human impact, good and bad, on the avian population. At the turn of the century, Great Egrets were nearly wiped out because people used their beautiful feathers to decorate hats. Thankfully, our fashion sense has

changed, and we humans realized the error of our ways. Conservation efforts have since resulted in a rebound of the egret populations.

Great Egrets have only recently become abundant in central Ohio due in part to the work of expanding and restoring the rivers around Columbus. Egrets are primarily considered a southern bird with 75% of the population thought to be in the swamps, bays, and rivers of states like Florida. The Great Egret's presence here in Ohio is truly a remarkable gift.

These herons have developed several adaptations that allow them to live in the Midwest where other herons do not. They eat only smaller fish and amphibians and are therefore not in competition with great blue herons. They also are not picky eaters and will stalk and strike pretty much any small tasty looking critters. Great Egrets rely on their social network to find good spots for feeding—where you see one bird, you will likely soon see more.

I can learn from the Great Egret's flexibility and adaptation. If—wait, I mean *when*—I am rigid in my thinking, I might try to solve a problem in the same way over and over. I am usually better off if I change course. Or I might choose to look at things from a different angle and seek input from my social network. In this manner, I can solve problems in a new way I might never have considered before. I can choose to be stubborn as a mule or flexible as a Great Egret.

> "WHAT IS MALLEABLE IS ALWAYS SUPERIOR TO THAT WHICH IS IMMOVABLE. THIS IS THE PRINCIPLE OF CONTROLLING THINGS BY GOING ALONG WITH THEM, OF MASTERY THROUGH ADAPTATION." — LAO TZU

Great Egret (Scioto Grove Metropark, June 2021)

18
GRAY CATBiRD

The Gray (or Grey) Catbird is another bird that you will often hear before you see—or sometimes only hear. It has a wide range of songs and calls and is related to mockingbirds. You will have to look carefully in dense bushes and lower tree branches once you hear the catbird's call in order to spot it. One of its more common vocalizations is said to sound like a cat's mewing. In my opinion, that interpretation is a stretch; they do not sound like any of the cats I have ever owned.

Catbirds typically eat insects in early summer, plant matter in fall, and wild berries in winter. Sometimes catbirds will dine at feeders, and according to Audubon.org, have been known to consume an odd assortment of human food such as doughnuts, cheese, boiled potatoes, and corn flakes. These foods do not seem odd to me, but I get the point that for a bird they are not so typical.

Gray Catbirds are tough. They respond to predators by flashing their wings and tails and even pecking at the interlopers if they get too close to the nest. A catbird will also destroy eggs of Brown-headed Cowbirds if laid in the catbird's nest. That seems reasonable to me.

The picture I took of the catbird does not look much like one would see if you Google the species. I believe this bird is actually molting and its feathers are being refreshed in preparation for migration. I did not realize that this stage is typical for many birds, particularly those getting ready to migrate south during the month of August. Birding in August tends to be a quiet activity and I just recently learned molting is one of the main reasons why. Who knew?

I debated putting this picture in the book since this catbird looks so different. Then I realized I was being too picky and holding on to my perfect ideal of a Gray Catbird's appearance. I finally decided this bird is simply perfect the way it is. When I let the need for "perfect" overtake what is "good," I can be frustrated with life. When I let life be what it is, molting feathers or not, I find more serenity in my days.

"GOOD ENOUGH IS THE NEW PERFECT."
– Becky Beaupre Gillespie

Gray Catbird (Clear Creek Metropark, September 2020)

20
BELTED KiNGFISHER

The Belted Kingfisher is the only variety of kingfisher that lives in Ohio. It can be found throughout the U.S. and into Mexico. The family includes over 90 species and is widely distributed across around the world. As a fishing bird, you will see it near lakes or rivers, perched as this one is on a branch waiting for its next meal to arrive.

A Belted Kingfisher's call is distinctive and worth learning to help spot it. Once you recognize their unusual, loud, dry, rattling call, you will often see them flying over the water. They are large birds of around 13 inches tall and both males and females are blue gray with white bellies. The "belt" refers to a blue-gray band across the bird's chest and the kingfisher female also has a second, rust-colored band. Females being more colorful than males is unusual in the bird world. You go, Belted Kingfisher girl!

Kingfishers are considered "antisocial." I had not previously heard that term used to describe bird behavior, but I have since realized that I only ever see one kingfisher at a time. Their call is in part a territorial warning to scare away competition. Pairs come together only to mate, build a nest, and raise their young. After those duties are completed, the birds part ways. They nest in underground tunnels and this picture may have been taken close to this proud father's brood of young.

Watching Belted Kingfishers fishing is an enjoyable pastime. They perch or hover above clear water for small fish, typically around 3 inches long. The bird sometimes also eats crustaceans, insects, reptiles, small mammals, or even other birds (!). Once they spot prey, kingfishers make a plunging headfirst dive into the water while closing their eyes to protect them from the impact.

The Belted Kingfisher taking a plunge is a good analogy for living life. I tend to be cautious and prefer to avoid risk. I do not dive in headfirst as much as I probably should. A Chinese proverb says, "Be not afraid of growing slowly; be afraid only of standing still." That is sound advice for a kingfisher.

"WHENEVER YOU FIND YOURSELF DOUBTING HOW FAR YOU CAN GO, REMEMBER HOW FAR YOU HAVE COME. REMEMBER EVERYTHING YOU HAVE FACED, ALL THE BATTLES YOU HAVE WON, AND ALL THE FEARS YOU HAVE OVERCOME." - N.R. WALKER

Belted Kingfisher (Scioto Bike Trail, July 2020)

YELLOW WARBLER

You may recall from Chapter 15 the Prothonotary Warbler with all of its orange, fiery plumage. As you can see from this photo, Yellow Warblers are also stunning—especially during breeding season. To distinguish the Yellow Warbler from the Prothonotary, the yellow has brown streaks on its breast, while the Prothonotary does not. Prothonotaries also have gray on their wings, while the yellows are solid...um, what is a synonym for "yellow"? I give up—yellow warblers are solid yellow.

Yellow Warblers are one of the earlier migrants back to their wintering grounds in Central and South America. They are typically packed up and have caught their flights by August. Correction—they have started to fly back, fortified by their summer of plentiful snacking on caterpillars, gnats, spiders, beetles, and wasps. Yum! Once the warblers arrive back in their winter homes, the birds can be found in mangrove forests and swamps.

When I took this picture the Yellow Warblers were everywhere. In May, many warblers spend a travel layover on the southern shores of Lake Erie. Many of them continue on to their final summer destination to breed in Canada. My friends and I were on the hunt to see how many different species of warblers we could spot at this location as well as if we could see any new types. I recall thinking I should not miss the chance to relish in the beauty of this guy, singing his heart out even if he was one of hundreds of birds all around me.

Similarly, I try to remember how each of us humans is remarkably precious. Even though there are billions of people, each of us has won the lottery to be alive today. And although we are in some ways alike, we are more unique than similar. No two of us have the same strengths, preferences, values, or appearances.

The Dalai Lama has said :

> "EVERY DAY, THINK AS YOU WAKE UP: 'TODAY I AM FORTUNATE TO BE ALIVE. I HAVE A PRECIOUS HUMAN LIFE. I AM NOT GOING TO WASTE IT.'"
>
> —DALAI LAMA

Thanks, Dalai Lama, and thanks, Yellow Warbler.

BONUS
FEMALE RUBY-THROATED HUMMiNGBiRD

You may already be thinking, "Hey, wasn't there already a chapter on Ruby-throated Hummingbirds?" Yes, yes, there was. But I am adding a bonus chapter on them because a) they are one of my favorite birds, b) as I write this chapter they are leaving Ohio, and c) I have the power of the pen.

What else should I say about Ruby-throats? These humming-birds sip nectar from tubular flowers with their long tongues which the birds actually store like a tape measure wrapped around inside their heads. That is a pretty cool trick!. I recommend planting tubular, red flowers when first starting to attract Ruby-throats because the more feeding options for them, the better. For example, I have had luck with red jewel salvia, red lobelia, and trumpet vine.

Hummingbirds typically hover while sipping nectar unless the feeder you provide has a perch. Their wings beat 50 times per second—try to tap your finger 50 times a second or do *anything* that fast. No luck? Give that bird some respect. If you are attempting to photograph and feed hummingbirds, the feeder's perch is a big help because otherwise the little buggers will not stay still for pictures.

When I took this photo, this gal was alternating between feeding from a lovely stand of bright orange jewel weed and resting. Can you tell she has her eyes closed? She was there for at least an hour or two and I attempted—and failed—many times to take her picture feeding in the jewel weed. I have so many pictures of blurry jewel weed. This was the best picture I got of her that particular weekend, and it seemed a fitting way to close my book. I may still eventually do a "blooper reel" chapter of bird picture failures.

The important thing was that no matter how many times I failed, I tried again. And even when I did not get exactly what I had set out to take, I was rewarded with a pretty damn good picture all the same.

> "THE GREATEST GLORY IN LIVING LIES NOT IN NEVER FAILING BUT IN RISING EVERY TIME WE FALL."
> - RALPH WALDO EMERSON

(above) Female Ruby-throated Hummingbird (Jackson Lake, September 2020)
(previous) Yellow Warbler (East Harbor State Park, May 2020)

BiRDiNG HACKS

iN THE BUCKEYE STATE

This chapter is meant to serve as a "how to" guide for beginning birders and photographers who, if you are like me, do not enjoy reading long, complex introductions to a new hobby. I am somewhat impatient by nature and learn things by trial and error.

Binoculars

Like pretty much every product out there today, you can spend a lot or a little on "binocs," but they are essential equipment for getting good bird sightings. If you are not sure you are going to like birding, you may want to start out with a smaller pair of binoculars that will run you in the neighborhood of $30 to $50. Of course, a pair like that will not be as powerful as if you spent a couple of hundred bucks on it. You could also borrow binocs from a friend or a local nature center just to get the hang of the technology. I do not recommend spending thousands of dollars, in any case. My pair of binoculars cost between $200 and $300 (it was a gift) and it works fine.

I got great instruction on how to use binocs during a free, guided bird walk at our local Audubon center. There are just a couple of adjustments to make to the binoculars to best fit your eyes and head, and I cannot effectively explain such an individual customization here. In my case, I simply turned the knobs willy nilly until I could see birds.

Practice using the binocs since it is trickier to master them than you may think. When you spot a bird, you want to have a decent sense of the markers surrounding it (e.g., how far the bird is from the trunk of the tree, if it is on a slender branch, etc.). Keep your eyes on the bird and bring the binocs to your eyes. That way you are less likely to lose your target.

You will have lots of failed sightings in the early going because birds sometimes fly away. (I know, shocker). A few bird species will stay still long enough to look at them and those can be a good starting place. Watching herons and great egrets, for example, can be rewarding because they typically move more slowly and are just gorgeous to peek at up close.

Since I like a challenge, I started with warblers who are as active as houseflies. That said, my solution was to go to a birding "hotspot"—a location that I knew would have lots of species to view. At a hotspot there were also other veteran birders who were happy to describe where to look and what type of birds were in the neighborhood.

Camera

I did not start taking pictures of birds right away. I wanted to learn their identities and how to use binoculars before I added that extra component. Even now I still find that taking a photo adds a bit of pressure for an outcome which can dilute the enjoyment of the moment.

Having said that, I do find it rewarding to take pictures—especially if I don't know what I am seeing. That way I can go back and identify the bird after the fact.

For the images in this book, I used my Canon PowerShot SX530. Early on I tried taking pictures with my phone, and while camera phones are amazing for up close and still pictures, they do not work well for bird photography. I would not spend more than a couple of hundred dollars for a digital camera and you can find sites with decent recommendations for beginners.

I received a book on bird photography as a gift and the first chapter said to "read your manual cover to cover." That is when I stopped reading that book. I still have a ton to learn about photography and I completely cheat by using automatic settings. That way the camera itself decides how to adjust settings and aperture. I still do not know what "aperture" means if I am being entirely honest. But I can take decent pictures letting the camera do the heavy lifting for me.

I figured out over time how to not have as many photography failures by understanding how to use light. In general, my eyes can tell me if a bird I am seeing is too deeply hidden in shade or leaves for a good picture. So, if I am out birding but not getting good photo opportunities because of the weather, I can still enjoy the bird sightings with my binoculars. On a sunny day, I look for places where birds are plentiful, and the sun can be behind me at my back. Sometimes this means scoping out a trail that allows for that approach. For example, in the morning, as the sun is rising in the east, a trail that goes north and has trees to my left (west) can provide great photo opportunities.

Finding Birds by Learning Their Calls

In many of the chapters, I mention birds you will likely hear before—or just as often as—you see them. I bet you already know more bird calls than you realize. Learning a few more can help you know when and where to start looking for birds.

While you can use any of the common birding websites such as eBird or Audubon.org to hear bird calls,the Ohio Department of Natural Resources (ODNR) offers a fantastic, free CD featuring audio of local birds. (Yes, my car still has a CD player in it!) You can go to your local ODNR office and pick up.this CD. I sometimes play it while traveling and just let it cycle through the calls, or before heading out I hone in on a particular species, such as warblers, to remind me what I might hear in the field.

Before you get overwhelmed by the hundred or so bird calls on the ODNR CD, I recommend beginners focus on learning the calls of the birds listed below that are not familiar to you now. (Note that not all of these birds are in this book, but they will likely be covered in future editions.)

Belted Kingfisher

Indigo Bunting

Yellow Warbler

Gray Catbird

Ruby-throated Hummingbird

Great Blue Heron

Cedar Waxwing

Northern Flicker

Baltimore Oriole

Whippoorwill

Finding Birds by Location

Early in my birding career, I thought I might see every bird in any setting. Okay, maybe that is an obvious exaggeration, but I did not realize how important location is when looking for birds. For example, despite plenty of open water, I have never seen any geese or great egrets at Lake Hope. Why? Scientists do not actually know. In general, there are "city birds" (pigeons, robins, cardinals, sparrows), "water birds," and "meadow birds." There are also special spots where I can find unique birds, like warblers on the south shore of Lake Erie in early May.

So how do I use this knowledge of bird locations? When I am planning a birding trip to a specific spot, I can prepare to see certain birds there and brush up on their calls. I will generally find catbirds in low bushes, swallows in the air, and starlings on wires. As I learn more of these location "hacks," I find more birds. That brings me to my next hack...

Finding Birds with eBird

I cannot say enough about how Cornell University's eBird website (https://ebird.org) has revolutionized birding for me and thousands of fellow "bird brains." I use the site to help me identify birds I have seen in a specific location, as well to determine which birds I want to see when planning a trip.

After I have been birding and taking pictures, I often have not fully identified some of the birds I saw. I made a mistake early in my birding career by bringing identification books on my trips, but later gave up on that approach so that I could enjoy my experiences (and not drag around more stuff in the field). I usually have some idea of a bird's identity, like a type of finch or thrush, when I see something in a particular location. I then check eBird to see what other birders have recently been spotting at that site. I also look at various species pictures to triangulate the evidence and come to a positive identification.

Rare bird alerts are another fun thing to read on eBird. I look at what species are showing up in Ohio and sometimes plan a trip to attempt to see a rare bird that has been spotted by other birders in a specific county. I have seen pelicans and the rare Ohio brown booby that way. That said, I have to be careful not to get excited and drive too far since the bird might fly away before I get there.

EPiLOGUE
BARRED OWL

The original picture I took of a Barred Owl was taken during a bike ride and was thus taken with my phone, so the quality was less than stellar. But imagine my excitement when I saw this fine feathered friend hanging out in the middle of the afternoon. The barred owl is also known as the swamp owl, striped owl, hoot owl, eight hooter, round-headed owl, and rain owl, according to naturemappingfoundation.org. I simply cannot make up this stuff!

Like many things I have thought about doing in life, I almost did not put this bird in my book because someday I might get a better picture. What? So my friends, I have named this the "Someday Owl," reminding me that life is too precious to put something off until tomorrow. Similarly, I was always going to write this book when I retired, when I had a less stressful job, when...whatever. I am so glad that I sat down and did it now. In case the space aliens land tomorrow, I have tackled one of my "someday owls," and it was a hoot.

Barred Owl (Olentangy Wetlands Bike Trail, June 2020)

ACKNOWLEDGMENTS

Thanks to my greatest fan base throughout my writing of this book—my family, especially my mom and daughters—for encouraging me to keep going. Thank you to the pre-publication reviewers of the manuscript, especially Austin for catching my buffleheaded mistakes. And thanks for the amazing work of my editor, John, and designer, Katie, for tirelessly answering my millions of questions.

SOURCES

I would like to recognize and thank the following sources I regularly referenced in the writing of this book, in addition to those directly cited in the preceding chapters:

Wikipedia https://www.wikipedia.org/

eBird https://ebird.org/home

Whatbird https://www.whatbird.com/

Cornell Lab https://www.allaboutbirds.org

Audubon https://www.audubon.org/bird-guide

Sibley, David Allen. Sibley Guide to Birds, Second Edition. Alfred A. Knopf, New York 2014

INDEX OF BiRDS

	Summer	Migration Celebration	Winter
American Coot		56	
American Crow			16
American Goldfinch			20
American Redstart		68	
American Robin			34
American Woodcock		38	
Bald Eagle			8
Baltimore Oriole	26		
Barred Owl	59		
Belted Kingfisher	46		
Black-crowned Night Heron	16		
Black-throated Blue Warbler		14	
Blue Jay			11
Brown Booby	20		
Bufflehead			37
Cedar Waxwing			40
Chickadee			18
Common Goldeneye			32
Common Tern		30	
Double-crested Cormorant	40		
Eastern Phoebe		46	
Evening Grosbeak		36	
Gray Catbird	44		
Great Blue Heron	32		
Great Egret	42		
Greater Yellowlegs	14		
Green-winged Teal		54	
Hermit Thrush		60	
Herring Gull	24		
Hooded Merganser			42

Horned Grebe		32	
House Finch			49
Indigo Bunting	30		
Merlin			44
Mute Swan	18		
Nashville Warbler		50	
Northern Cardinal			13
Northern Flicker			57
Northern Mockingbird			28
Northern Parula		18	
Northern Shoveler		64	
Palm Warbler		12	
Pied-billed Grebe		16	
Pileated Woodpecker	10		
Prothonotary Warbler	38		
Purple Martin	22		
Red-headed Woodpecker			30
Red-tailed Hawk			54
Ring-billed Gull			23
Ruby-throated Hummingbird	12, 50	42	
Ruddy Duck	34		
Rusty Blackbird		22	
Snowy Owl			26
Surf Scoter		20	
Tree Swallow	36		
Trumpeter Swan	18		
Tufted Titmouse			52
Turkey Vulture	28		
White-throated Sparrow			47
Wood Duck		70	
Yellow-rumped Warbler		10	
Yellow Warbler	48	26	

www.ingramcontent.com/pod-product-compliance
Lightning Source LLC
Chambersburg PA
CBHW071941260326
41914CB00004B/708